Simply Mindful

Simply Mindful

A Daily Practice to Reclaim Your Life

Albert Bellg

Appleton, Wisconsin

Copyright © 2019 Albert Bellg

All rights reserved. If you copy or quote parts of this book or the mindful practice exercises, please do so with proper attribution. Thank you for respecting the work that has gone into this book.

Sloan Press/LifePath ❀
1620 S. Lawe St., Suite 4
Appleton, Wisconsin 54915
Sloan Press is an imprint of LifePath LLC
Simply Mindful is a trademark of LifePath LLC

ISBN 978-0-9965103-5-6
eISBN 978-0-9965103-6-3
Library of Congress Control Number: 2017913968

Interior design by Albert Bellg.
Cover design by Mary Ann Smith.
Cover photo by Marcus Gann, licensed through Shutterstock.
Set in Arno Pro by Renana Typesetting.

*This book is for my family
and for all of us looking for peace and insight
when life gets difficult.*

Contents

Foreword by Dr. Bruce Rybarczyk — ix
Introduction: Living in the Tragic Gap — xi

Chapter 1: A Simple Daily Practice — 1
Chapter 2: Let Go of Tension — 15
Chapter 3: Reduce Distractibility — 27
Chapter 4: Practice Everywhere — 39
Chapter 5: Make Mindful Choices — 49
Chapter 6: Toward a Mindful Life — 57

Gratitude — 65
Notes, Comments and References — 67
About the Author — 75

Foreword

Dr. Bellg has done it again. He has put his considerable gifts of writing in a personal, readable and concise manner toward creating a practical mindfulness guidebook for everyone and anyone. Psychologists like myself are always in search of useful guides to get clients and patients started on their journey of improving their lives, and this is an excellent place to start.

Dr. Bellg uses his own personal experience in practicing and teaching meditation for decades to pass along practical strategies as well as pearls of wisdom about how practicing breath awareness creates its remarkable effects. He leads the reader through the different exercises he has field-tested personally and professionally and does so without introducing any of the jargon that is so often espoused by those with his level of experience.

I will gladly recommend it to my own patients as a starting place for learning one of the great skills for wellness.

>Dr. Bruce Rybarczyk, Professor
>Psychology Department
>Virginia Commonwealth University
>Richmond, Virginia

Introduction

Living in the Tragic Gap

In the middle of the journey of my life, I awoke and found myself in a dark wood where the straight way was lost.
— DANTE ALIGHIERI

Eleanor was a woman in her early seventies. She walked slowly, slightly stooped, and her face looked strained and defeated. Her husband had died a couple of years earlier, and she was living alone in the small house that they had shared for forty-five years. His life insurance had enabled her to pay off what remained of the last mortgage they'd had to take out on it, and with a bit of savings she was financially able to make ends meet. She had a garden with flowers and a few vegetables, and a small patio under a tree where she could sit in the shade and read on a sunny day.

Then some new neighbors moved into the house next door. They had loud voices and liked to play loud music. When she asked them to turn it down, they sometimes did the opposite. They had friends with motorcycles who came roaring up to visit them at all hours. They sometimes threw things over the fence, or made rude comments when they saw her in her garden. She felt intimidated and afraid. Even when they weren't around, she was still apprehensive about going outside, and she couldn't sit and read in her back yard without feeling distracted and anxious.

Although the harassment wasn't constant, she was always afraid that it would resume. She kept the windows to her house closed tight so she couldn't hear their voices and music, even in the summer when her poorly insulated house, which had no air conditioning, became dangerously hot. She felt powerless and helpless. She also had no energy left to do the volunteer activities in her community that meant a lot to her. But she didn't want to move from her home and the many good memories it held, and she felt trapped.

I met her when she came to one of the first mindful meditation classes I taught after becoming a psychologist. In answer to the question "Why do you want to learn to meditate?" that I usually ask everyone at the beginning of the first class, she commented briefly on having a lot of stress in her life but didn't say much more than that. I learned her story when she took me aside after the last class and told me the details. I was sympathetic and supportive, but she was dealing with a very difficult situation. Frankly, I didn't see how she could solve her problem without moving.

To my surprise, though, a few months later she showed up in another meditation class. There was a spring in her step and she was smiling, clearly in better spirits. A few weeks later when that class was finished, she again took me aside to talk.

"I wanted you to know that things are going better for me," she said. "I was standing at the sink washing dishes a couple of weeks ago, I had the windows open, and suddenly realized I was singing like I used to. I feel like I've gotten my life back."

That's great, I said. So the people next door have moved?

"No, they're still there, still loud, sometimes," she said. "But I'm different. They don't get to me the way they used to. I'm not afraid to do the things I want to do around the house and in my yard, and I get out more. I'm free. And I'm happy, at least some of the time. Things are still difficult, but it's better. I just wanted you to know."

Like Eleanor, sooner or later most of us will run into a challenge that turns our life upside down.

Whether it's a medical problem, a change in our personal life, the loss of a loved one, a crisis at work, a financial or legal problem, or simply the ongoing stress of daily life that becomes too much to bear, at some point we'll likely become overwhelmed and unable to cope.

Or it might even be worse. Circumstances may make it impossible to fulfill our own or others' expectations about the work we do or our family role. We may no longer enjoy the activities and relationships that give our life meaning. Perhaps we lose confidence and self-respect. Or we may lose control over what matters to us, and feel that our life is no longer our own.

If that happens – *when* that happens – we'll find ourselves experiencing the tension, stress and even grief in the space between *what can be* and *what is,* what we want for our life and the limits that our circumstances dictate. Author and educator Parker Palmer calls this "living in the tragic gap," and from my own experience, I know that it's a difficult place to be. When we face a major life challenge that hits us personally, we usually live closer to the painful *what is* than the hopeful *what can be,* particularly if we're unable to change what's happening.

In those situations, can we find a way through tension, stress and grief? Can we reclaim what's meaningful about life?

Many things in this world can't be changed. But as Eleanor found, sometimes *we* can change. Surprisingly, we can often change our response to adversity in a way that not only enables us to handle it better, but also lets us see our situation with greater perspective and clarity. We might also see ourselves more clearly and be better able to act on what matters to us.

For example, as a health psychologist over the last two decades, I've worked with medical patients, professionals, family caregivers, and others dealing with medical and personal problems that completely changed their lives. As impossible as it might have seemed initially, many of them found a way to live successfully despite their challenges.

Mindful practice was often an important part of what they did to live with *what is* and move as best they could toward *what can be.* In the face of daunting circumstances, mindful practice helped them – and can help anyone – see and respond to situations more realistically, making them neither too large nor too small. It can help us defuse some of the powerful feelings and negative thoughts we have about what's happening to us. Being mindful also helps us to stay real and face what's happened without trying to manipulate ourselves into thinking "happy thoughts" that feel like lies. It lets us choose how much of our life is involved with our problems, and how much we focus on who and what we love. It gives us a choice about the attitude we take toward our life.

Mindful practice also makes it possible to think differently about ourselves. When serious life problems show up, we might think that it's our fault or that there's something wrong with us. Maybe we accuse ourselves of being "weak" or blame ourselves for not doing what we think we should have done to avoid the problem. Or we may believe or hear from others that we should "snap out of it." As most of us know, the pressure to pretend that nothing's wrong and live up to unrealistic expectations makes the stress we're experiencing even worse.

In contrast to such critical self-judgment, mindful practice opens the door to seeing clearly and accepting what's happened to us with compassion for our imperfect humanity, just as we might offer caring and understanding to others in a similar situation. Far from being "self-indulgent" or "weak," research shows that genuine compassion for our own humanity actually allows us to be more resilient in dealing with ongoing difficulties.

I have learned a lot from people facing life-changing difficulties with courage. It has been humbling to work with people whose medical problems or life circumstances force them to live on the edge, yet who still offer care and compassion for themselves and others. Where I've included stories from such remarkable people in this book, I've changed some of the details to preserve their privacy and anonymity.

I deeply appreciate how mindful practice can help us clarify what matters. It can help us create the undistracted attention we need to cultivate the relationships, activities, and ways of being that most deeply express our values, joys and sense of purpose. Whatever tragic gap we may be standing in, mindful practice can help us reconnect with who we are and what we truly care about.

Albert Bellg
Appleton, Wisconsin
April, 2019

Chapter 1

A Simple Daily Practice

Breath... unites your body to your thoughts.
— THÍCH NHẤT HẠNH

Mindful practice may seem simple. But when I first tried to do it, I couldn't.

I was a skinny, bushy-haired twenty-year-old, painfully self-conscious, constantly worried about almost everything except what I knew best, being a student and playing soccer.

I was getting ready to graduate from college, and I was scared and more than a little overwhelmed when I realized I had to live in the world and support myself. What I'd read about Transcendental Meditation (TM was the popular form of meditation at the time) seemed promising: it claimed to help people calm their minds and reduce anxiety and stress. College students got a special discount, so I signed up.

In a quiet, dimly lit room with the shades drawn in the student union on campus, I was given a mantra (a Sanskrit word I didn't understand) and told to sit and repeat it over and over to myself. I tried my best. What I found, though, was that I couldn't be still.

My mind wandered and I was too physically restless to relax. After a few days, I quit.

A couple of years later, though, I found a way to meditate that worked better for me: the gentle movements of t'ai chi. As I started taking lessons, I found that there were physical activities and sensations to focus on – and I surprised myself by being able to do that. I also learned that t'ai chi consciously linked the slow movements of the form with the even slower rhythm of my breath. T'ai chi made it possible for me to meditate for the first time in my life.

Fast forward through several decades of practicing various forms of meditation and mindful practice, and teaching it to individuals and groups struggling with stress, anxiety, depression, medical problems and other life issues. I still do several different meditative and contemplative practices, but at least once a day I do the simple mindful exercise described below. Like my early successful experience with t'ai chi, it combines awareness of a gentle physical experience with a simple and straightforward response to being distracted.

As an anxious, distractible college student, my own difficulty in finding a way to slow down and focus inwardly kept me from meditating successfully for many years. So I sympathize with people who find meditation and mindful practice challenging. Yet if I'd known that there were other ways to pursue a mindful practice besides what I was originally taught (TM), it would have been far easier for me to get started. So as we begin, I want to make this process easier than it was for me. I also would like to offer a better understanding than I had about why mindful practice – particularly the practice described next – is helpful.

❊ A Simple Daily Practice

Sit in a comfortable position.

Focus your attention on your breath, just as it is.

When distracted, bring attention back to your breath.

Do this for about ten minutes, once or twice a day.

Why this?

It turns out that there are lots of ways to practice being mindful, maybe as many types of *meditation* as there are *medication*, as I sometime tell the medical patients I work with. So why do this one?

What we pay attention to – what we're *mindful* of – makes a difference. If we spend several hours listening to the news on television, we're likely to get pretty upset and wound up. If we spend the same amount of time in the woods, listening to the wind in the trees and a stream making its way over rocks, we'll be calmer and more peaceful. If we do either of those things regularly, we'll learn a habitual way of being that will affect the broad experience we have of our life and the world.

Similarly, we can learn to make choices that affect our experience of a specific crisis or stressful situation. Ideally, we'd like to choose how much attention we give to it, how much it distresses us, how we think and feel about it, what we're going to do about it, and how we keep it in balance with more positive aspects of our life. Making such choices is far easier said than done – but a regular mindful practice helps us cultivate new habits (and break old ones) that can make those choices possible, at least some of the time.

The simple daily practice above asks us to pay attention to two experiences that make a difference in our physical and emotional reactivity and in our ability to focus on the things that are important to us. As it happens, taking even a few minutes of each day to be mindful of these quite ordinary experiences can powerfully change our life.

The first experience is our breath. Breathing is a gentle rhythm that is relaxing when we pay attention to it. The first Western researchers who studied meditation back in the 1960's were looking for the "active ingredient" in meditation that helped people relax. They found that one of the key elements was repetition, being aware of the gentle rhythm of our breath or a repeated mantra. It's similar to how we feel when we're near a lake or an ocean listening to the slow rhythm of the waves coming in. When we pay attention to the slow pace of our normal breathing, our mind and body naturally let go of tension and relax.

The second part of this simple mindful practice consists of turning our attention away from distractions – thoughts, feelings, physical sensations and sounds – and focusing back on our breath. Distractions in daily life can be stressful and sometimes hard to ignore. They also frequently keep us from being able to concentrate on things we care about. During the time we're engaged in this mindful practice, no matter how insistent a sensation or sound may be, or how important a distracting thought is to us, we turn our attention away from it and back to our breath.

As we shift attention back to our breath when we're distracted, we turn away from something that stresses our mind and body and toward something that relaxes us. We also weaken our old habit of being distracted by anything that comes along and reinforce a new habit of focusing on what we care about. As we continue to practice turning away from distractions during the exercise, we are learning a skill that makes it easier to pay attention to what's truly important in daily life: the person in front of us, the task that requires our complete concentration, or something else that genuinely matters.

Mindful practice FAQ

So if this simple mindful practice is about letting go of tension and relaxing, doesn't it make sense to lie down when I practice?

Actually, no. When we're in bed, being aware of our breathing, setting aside distractions and letting our body relax can make it easier to go to sleep. But for the most part, we've already learned to relax while we're lying down, and what's not so easy is to relax while we're awake and sitting up. Doing the simple mindful practice while sitting will make it easier to relax in other situations (at work or school, perhaps) when we may be sitting and stressed.

What about letting myself fall asleep when I'm doing it?

Similarly, as tempting as it may be, it's not a good idea to fall asleep while doing the mindful practice. Most of us are better at relaxing and falling asleep than we are at relaxing and staying awake – and what we're learning with this mindful practice is how to be relaxed while we're awake and alert! So we try not to fall asleep during practice.

Wouldn't it help me relax if I deliberately made my breath deeper or slower?

As for letting our breath be just as it is, there's a reason for that, too. Some meditation or relaxation practices suggest that we give equal time to the in-breath and out-breath, breathe in sync with a timer, breathe with pauses, slow down our breathing, breathe deeply, or breathe diaphragmatically from the lower part of our body. There are good reasons to practice controlling our breath in those ways. However, our regular breathing, just as it is without us trying to control it, has the advantage of telling us something about our body's present state. Are we tense or anxious? Are we feeling sad, numb or overwhelmed? Our thoughts and feelings show up in how we breathe: slow or fast, shallow or deep, tight or with more freedom. As we become mindful of how thoughts and feelings affect the way we breathe, we can use that awareness to understand ourselves better and change how we react.

What if I get an itch? Or suddenly remember something important I definitely don't want to forget?

In this simple mindful practice, we consider every thought, feeling or sensation (except for breathing) a distraction. But if something really important suddenly comes to mind, it's fine to take a moment to write it down and then return to mindful practice. That's better than having the additional distraction of worrying about forgetting it. Similarly, if there's an itch, I suggest scratching it. Then go back to the practice. This is not what every mindfulness teacher recommends, and there are quite excellent reasons for recommending a different response to distractions (for example, breathing into discomfort and seeing if we can let it go). To start, though, I suggest doing what we need to do about an important distraction and then returning attention to the breath.

Why can't I just relax doing something else?

There are many other ways to relax besides meditation. So, as I've heard many people suggest, why not listen to music, read a book, take a nap, or go for a walk? Or take a vacation?

Those are certainly good things to do and they improve our quality of life, but they tend to work only while we're doing them. Almost everyone has experienced the positive effects of a vacation "wearing off" within a few days of returning to their daily routine. As much as we might enjoy and benefit from listening to music, reading, taking a nap, or going for a walk in our neighborhood, the effect of those activities is temporary.

Mindful practice, however, does more than give us a break or distract us from circumstances that are stressful or distressing. Like a regular physical workout, it is a training that gives us the ability to respond to our daily experiences in a different way. Just as a physical exercise routine will, over time, improve our strength or cardiovascular conditioning and benefit us in daily activities whenever we need to be a bit stronger or have more stamina, a regular routine of mindful practice will change our habitual or conditioned patterns of stress and emotional reactivity during daily life.

So if we do mindful practice regularly and in a variety of situations (as we'll discuss later), we'll be more relaxed and focused in a broad range of stressful and difficult circumstances. A simple daily mindful practice will affect our life in a deep and lasting way.

What to expect

After a couple of weeks of mindful practice, most of us will start to notice some specific changes – again, just as we would a few weeks after starting a physical workout routine. But in this case, perhaps we'll be less angry when we're driving and someone cuts us off in traffic, or more patient with people who get on our nerves. Or we may find it easier to do everyday chores without so much inner struggle, or get greater satisfaction from work we enjoy. Or if we're in chronic pain or discomfort, we may find it easier to stay focused on the things we want to do and not let our activities be impaired as much by our pain.

For some people, however, it may take longer to see a benefit or feel that "it's working." If someone does hard physical labor, is under chronic physical or emotional stress, or is experiencing significant anxiety or depression, the patterns of tension that they've learned may be deeply ingrained and they may take longer to feel a change from mindful practice. It also may take more time if someone is a heavy drinker, a smoker, uses recreational drugs or takes prescription medications that tend to blunt awareness of the body or emotions. If it takes a bit longer to unlearn old patterns of tension and experience the benefits I've described, I encourage patience and persistence: stick with the practice and see what happens.

Mindful practice can help people feel calmer, which might make it easier to cut back on alcohol or recreational drugs if that's a choice that seems right. However, for people taking medication for clinical anxiety or depression, it's important to keep taking the medications and do mindful practice in addition to it. Mindful practice is one of the very best things we can do to supplement medical treatment and improve symptoms of anxiety and depression.

Is there a downside to watch for? In my experience, a small percentage of people (maybe one to two percent) starting a meditation or relaxation practice may find the awareness of physical relaxation strange, slightly disorienting, or "just not who they are." For those who experience a mild version of this and are willing to continue, I'd suggest practicing for short periods (a minute or two) until the experience of meditating and being relaxed becomes more familiar.

It is also possible, though rare (I've experienced this with only two people in two decades) that learning to relax the physical tension we've been holding releases emotions, sometimes powerful emotions, and difficult or painful memories associated with those feelings. If that happens, I'd suggest stopping mindful practice (at least for a while) and seeking out a psychologist or counselor who can help explore those feelings. As a psychologist, I can say with confidence that although it's true that "you can't change the past" (as many people have told me when they try to dismiss psychotherapy as an option for themselves), it is almost always possible to change how much the past affects our present life.

A larger percentage of people, however, will find that the first few sessions of mindful practice will lead to them feeling exhausted. This may initially seem discouraging – why practice something that makes us feel tired? – but the exhaustion typically eases after a few weeks of regular practice and people actually start to feel more energized. Why would some people feel wrung out at all, though?

Many people who feel tired when they start mindful practice are actually pushing themselves hard to get through their day. When they start to meditate, the relaxation it evokes releases them from the emotional pressure, stress and urgency they have learned to live with, and they discover how truly tired they are when they're not mercilessly driving themselves. The good news is that after a few weeks of regular practice, their natural inner resources are usually restored. At that point, they find that mindful practice helps them be more physically relaxed, mentally focused and energized, almost as if they'd taken a nap. They're likely to be more productive as well.

For most of us, though, mindful practice will be comfortable and relaxing from the start, and make it easier to handle daily difficulties. After practicing for a while, we'll also find that we've created a tool we can use intentionally to change our reaction to specific difficult circumstances. The tool we develop – the ability to relax deeply by taking a conscious breath – can be used any time we want to change how we're handling a stressful situation, even when we're face-to-face with someone. We'll talk more about how that works later on.

Can ten minutes a day really help?

Does practicing ten minutes a day really make a difference? That's a fair question, given that the practice I recommend takes that much time out of the day. Based on my experience of teaching mindful practice and the positive results I've seen, as well as the many research studies that show meditation and mindful practice to be one of the most effective behavioral interventions there is, I am confident that it does make a difference, often a profound one. Having seen those benefits in my life and others, I know that investing ten minutes every day in mindful practice is one of the most worthwhile things we can do, especially when we're facing a serious life challenge.

For me, the more intriguing question is: why does it work so well? How can a ten-minute exercise be so powerful and lead to so many positive changes? If we do the math, ten minutes is just one percent of the time we're awake. How can something we do for one percent of our day act as a counterbalance to sixteen or more waking hours of feeling stressed or overwhelmed? What makes mindful practice so powerful?

The way I've come to think of it, mindful practice is less a counterbalance to the rest of our day and more like what a physical therapist would call a "range of motion" exercise. In physical rehabilitation, we gently stretch a muscle or rotate a joint that is restricted in its movement out to the limits of its motion. We don't have to do it for a long period of time. We get the ongoing benefits of increased flexibility and reduced pain simply by moving a limb to the outer limit of its range several times a day, gradually extending our range of motion as the days go by.

In a similar way, we can consider a ten-minute daily period of mindful practice as a *range of tension* exercise. For ten minutes, we focus on our breath and let go of physical, emotional and mental tension we ordinarily never release. That extends the range of how relaxed we can be. More importantly, it starts to break up our ongoing learned patterns of stress and emotional reactivity. Our response to stressful events may become less intense and shorter, and we may also feel less tension throughout the day.

With that in mind, there is nothing particularly magical or necessary about a ten-minute period of practice. Most people find that ten minutes allows them to feel as relaxed as they're going to feel, and to change our learned pattern of tension it's important to get as close as we can to the relaxed end of our range of tension at least once a day and stay there for a while. But if five minutes is the only length of time that fits the schedule on a particular day, we can do five minutes. Or if fifteen or twenty minutes feels good, we can do that.

For many people whom I've taught this practice, finding time is less a scheduling problem than one of priorities. Do we *really* not have the ability to choose what to do with one percent of our day? What does that say about our life if we find ourselves trapped by that belief?

For most people, finding time for something they care about is more a creative challenge than a logistical one. There are plenty of opportunities during the day to take a few minutes to practice (during television commercials, while we're waiting in line at the grocery store, during a walk, etc.). It's just making the commitment to recognize and use them.

Do it comfortably

Finally, remember that the first instruction is, "Sit in a comfortable position." Note that the first mindful task is to determine what's a comfortable way to sit and what isn't – and perhaps that may lead us to wonder why we weren't in a comfortable position already. As we mindfully observe or witness the rest of our experience, we might also start to notice other uncomfortable ways we live.

Another important message is this: we need to practice in a way that works for each of us. There are many possibilities for how long we do this practice (for example, ten minutes once a day, five minutes twice a day), where we do it (in our bedroom, at the kitchen table, in the restroom, sitting in our car), and even how we do it. The best mindful practice is the one we actually do. If we're going to make this regular practice part of our daily routine, let's do it in a way we can easily live with.

For many years, the above simple daily practice was all I taught and recommended. But if we explore and incorporate what's to come in the following chapters, the practice will be easier to do, more effective and – perhaps surprisingly – less difficult to fit into the day. The rest of this book is about improving the effects of mindful practice, doing it in ways that fit into our daily routine without disrupting it, and using it to change our attitude toward the life challenges that come our way.

Summary

This simple mindful practice...

- Focuses awareness on a naturally relaxing experience, the gentle rhythm of our breath.

- Lets us notice what the natural pattern of our breathing tells us about our physical and emotional state.
- Gives us practice shifting our attention away from distractions.
- Has many positive effects on our daily life, just as a regular routine of physical exercise does.
- Helps us create a tool to use in specific stressful and difficult situations.
- Is a "range of tension" exercise that offers benefits far greater than the ten minutes or so we spend doing it.
- Works best when we do it regularly, so we need to fit it into our routine in a way that's comfortable.

Chapter 2

Let Go of Tension

Letting go does not mean not caring about things. It means caring about them in a flexible and wise way.

– JACK KORNFIELD

Larry was a commodities trader at the Chicago Board of Trade a couple of miles down the freeway from where I worked at the Rush Heart Institute. He was tall, intense and impatient. Like many of the traders there, he came to our clinic because he was trying to avoid heart problems. His high cholesterol and blood pressure put him at serious risk of a heart attack or stroke. Those conditions were being treated medically by our preventive cardiology team, but he was referred to me for something else: his uncontrolled anger with his family.

"I don't get it," he said. "In the last six months, I go home and I'm shouting at my wife, angry with my kids – I hardly recognize myself. I'm sure they don't either."

Has anything changed in your life in the last six months? I asked him.

"No, not really. Well… I had a falling-out with a couple of guys I work with who I thought were 'friends' until they tried to screw me out of some fees that were rightfully mine. But my job is still good, and I get a charge out of staying on top of things and trading. I'm a 'type A' person, and proud of it – it's made me a success!"

Are there other things you're not enjoying as much as you have in the past?

"Funny you should ask. I have this great sailboat, a thirty-two footer, and I used to go out on the lake on weekends with my family, or maybe invite a few friends from work. I haven't had it out for months. Just no interest."

Is it hard to fall asleep or to stay asleep?

"Yeah, both. I just can't get my brain to turn off when I get into bed, and I sometimes wake up at night, maybe around two a.m., and can't fall back for a couple of hours."

We talked a while more, and then I suggested he might want to try reducing his stress by doing a regular mindful practice. I also told him he might have some mild clinical depression, and that mindful practice sometimes helps that, too. But he didn't even want to talk about stress, let alone depression.

"I'm not stressed," he insisted. "I get a kick out of my job, can't wait to get there in the morning. And forget about taking another medicine for your so-called 'depression' – I've got enough with all these heart pills."

OK, I said. But there's something going on that's making you irritable and hard to live with at home. Let's give mindful practice a try and see what happens. We'll know whether we're on the right track in a couple of months.

We met a few more times, and he finally had a verdict for mindful practice. "I have to say, I didn't think much was going to happen," he said. "I've been pushing to get things done all my life, *ever since I was a kid. But I know things are going better at home, and I'm not shouting anymore. My wife is noticing – I think she noticed before I did – and she keeps encouraging me to stick with this breathing thing you gave me to do."*

He smiled wryly. *"We've even been out on the boat the last couple of weekends. Who knew I could have such a good time hanging out with my kids for an afternoon?"*

It's not always easy to know when we're stressed or burned out. As it was with Larry, everything may seem fairly normal, but our body and mind may experience substantial stress that we're not even aware of. Maybe we're minimizing the conflicts and pressures at work, tiptoeing apprehensively around family problems without resolving them, or worrying about medical issues but not doing anything about them. Then, like the proverbial frog not noticing that it's slowly being heated up in a pan of water, we suddenly realize something's different – and very wrong. Maybe we're sad, crying and anxious, or overwhelmed and numb, or irritable and angry like Larry. We aren't ourselves anymore and can't stop feeling that way. Like the frog, we're cooked.

The stress we can't see

Most of the stress and tension we experience doesn't feel like stress and tension at all. It just feels normal. For example, Larry thought that the normal pressures of his job were stimulating and positive, which they clearly were for him, at least in part. But they put him right up against the edge of his ability to cope, and he was pushed over that line by his health problems and relationships at work.

It's not hard to see how this happens. Over time, we can get used to how we respond to stressful experiences and no longer see them as problems. But our body doesn't get used to them. Even if we're no longer aware of them, our pattern of stress reactions take a toll, which may show up as compassion fatigue (which is when we feel too tired or cynical to care anymore), emotional exhaustion, irritability, depersonalization of the people we're supposed to be helping, lack of satisfaction with our life or work, or burnout (which is a combination of several of these symptoms).

Unfortunately, there's also another level to this: the response we're taught to have to "normal" stress reactions may be to dismiss what we're feeling. "Suck it up," we may tell ourselves, having heard it from others. Or another favorite: "Just get on with it." Our regional culture (especially where I live, in the upper Midwest) often imposes the unspoken demand that we deliberately ignore being sick, stressed or emotionally upset. Or that unspoken demand might be gender related: men in our culture are pressured not to show signs of pain, injury or weakness, and women are often diminished and considered weak when they show emotion. Some professional cultures also insist that personal illness or fatigue be ignored, which contributes to the fact that over half of all physicians in the United States have at least one sign of serious burnout.

Finally, just to make stress even more difficult to identify, the "normal" level of tension, anxiety, irritability and other signs of stress that we experience may even become a proud part of our identity. We may enjoy being a driven but successful "type A" business person like Larry, a busy multi-tasker who loves to do five things at the same time, or a perfectionist who must do the job exactly right even if they have to stay up until two a.m.

What with becoming desensitized to stressful experiences, cultural and internal pressures to deny our stress, and making chronic stress a part of our identity, it's not surprising that a significant part of the stress and tension we have in our body and mind throughout the day is invisible to our ordinary awareness.

This has important implications for daily practice. Limiting mindful practice to times when we are actually aware of feeling stressed or tense only addresses the most severe stress and reactivity that is outside our normal unconscious stress pattern. It doesn't change our broader, mostly invisible daily pattern of stress and reactivity. So we need to do mindful practice regularly to reduce the stress reactions we're not aware of, even on vacation or when we're feeling that everything's fine.

If I haven't been quite convincing about the existence of invisible stress and tension, notice that nearly everyone becomes more relaxed after doing the simple mindful practice for a few minutes, even if they think they already feel relaxed. In other words, by doing the mindful exercise, nearly all of us are aware that we let go of tension we didn't feel before we started.

Here's another way to become aware of invisible tension and let it go with just a few breaths.

※ Let the Center of Your Breathing Sink

Find the place in your chest or belly that feels like the center of your breathing, the place where your breath is coming from.

Without forcing it in any way, let the center of your breathing sink. It may move a little, a lot, or not at all.

If it moves, notice how you feel different or how your breathing changes. You've just let go of tension that you hadn't been aware of.

After you've practiced this for a while, you'll find that you can let the center of your breathing sink farther and release even more tension.

Reducing invisible stress

The exercise above reveals invisible tension in a clear and simple way. It's a kind of biofeedback exercise, without all the usual biofeedback technology. Biofeedback makes us aware of a physiological process in our body that we're ordinarily oblivious to, such as our blood pressure, skin conductivity, heart rate, muscle tension, or brain function. The technology that senses and measures those physical processes then offers us "feedback" on them that is either visual (perhaps with a light, a number, a line on a graph, or a change in a visual scene) or audible (with a beep or some other sound).

Remarkably, nearly everyone finds that they can change the underlying physiological process that the equipment reveals by simply *intending* for the feedback they're receiving to change. With regular practice over time, these changes can be significant and lasting. People can learn to lower their blood pressure, calm their heart rate, and reduce physiological signs of stress.

That's what the exercise above can help us do, too, but without all the wires and feedback gear. Think of it as a zero-tech biofeedback exercise. By discovering what feels like the "center of our breathing," we become aware of the invisible pattern of tension creating that experience in our chest or belly. When we're tense, the center of our breathing tends to be higher in our body. When we're relaxed, it's lower. By letting the center of our breathing sink, we're changing a pattern of tension that we hadn't been aware of.

It's rather remarkable that this works to let go of tension even after we've been meditating for five or ten minutes. We're certainly more relaxed after mindfully focusing on our breath for a while. But we're still tense in ways we're not aware of, and some of that tension lets go when we let the center of our breathing sink.

So at least once or twice during every mindful practice session, it's good to check in on the center of our breathing and let it sink. It helps us become aware of and release tension that's hard to notice in the moment, and it also weakens our ongoing habits and patterns of tension.

Our heart rate varies

For several years, I taught health psychology at Lawrence University in Appleton, Wisconsin. One of my favorite class demonstrations was to show students how to change their heart rate variability (HRV).

Everyone knows that our heart rate goes up when we're exercising, anxious or stressed, and it goes down when we're relaxed. But HRV is something else. Our heart rate and breathing actually affect each other: when we inhale, our heart rate temporarily goes up, and when we exhale, it goes down. The difference between the lower and higher rates can be quite significant, as much as 25 or so beats per minute. But, typically, we don't notice the change. When we check our pulse, it's usually for a length of time that covers several breaths and many heartbeats, so the variability averages out. But the fact that our heart rate and breath are connected makes HRV a sensitive indicator of stress.

In the class demo, I connected a student volunteer to biofeedback sensors that detected their breathing and the beat-to-beat rate of their heart, and then projected the graph of those two numbers on a screen for the entire class to observe. When I asked the volunteer to imagine being in a relaxing location, the image on the screen usually looked something like this:

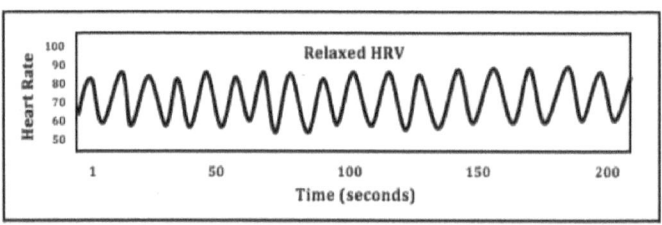

The beat-to-beat heart rate in this diagram gracefully increases and decreases with the person's breath. In this case, the maximum in-breath to out-breath variability is quite large (up to 25 or so beats per minute), which is usually a sign of someone healthy or young, or both.

Then I'd ask the volunteer to make one change. I'd say: *Continue to breathe regularly, but instead of imagining yourself in a relaxing location, think about the next test you're studying for or the next paper you have due.*

When they changed what they were thinking about, the student didn't look or feel different. Their overall heart rate didn't necessarily go up very much, either. But by changing just what they were thinking about, their heart rate variability showed that their body and nervous system were reacting strongly to what they were thinking.

Even a mildly stressful thought about a school assignment or test that they experienced every day made the simple, regular association between their breath and heart rate disappear and had a dramatic effect on their heart rate variability. This

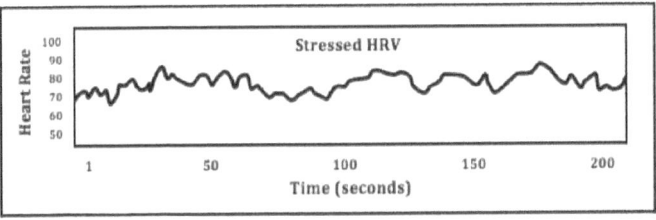

lead to an equally dramatic conclusion to the demonstration, when I was able to say, with the evidence in front of them: even our thoughts have the power to change how our body functions.

But what happens when we're chronically worried or stressed, day after day after day? The pattern of stress becomes chronic, too. We develop an ongoing pattern of stress symptoms that becomes "normal" and is with us all the time – and certain aspects of our HRV change in an ongoing way as well, even at times when we think we're relaxed.

The good news is that when we do a regular mindful practice and break the pattern of chronic stress, our HRV can return to a non-stressed state. The even better news is that it matters.

Heart rate variability is a risk factor for heart disease. People who have HRV patterns associated with chronic stress are at higher risk of having a heart attack, of developing coronary artery disease, and of having a heart rhythm disruption. It makes sense that if external stressors affect our health risks, they will also have a measurable effect on physiological processes. HRV shows clearly how our thoughts, feelings and health are linked.

HRV is not the only health risk indicator that is improved by mindful practice. Our health is also at risk from inflammation (particularly in the coronary arteries, where inflammation accelerates the accumulation of plaque), high blood pressure, "sticky platelets" that increase our chance of a blood clot, elevated stress hormones, anxiety, depression, negative relationships, social isolation, and other factors. Mindful practice can directly or indirectly improve many of these health risks.

So it's good to do mindful practice when we're not feeling stressed. Mindful practice reduces health risks and changes broad patterns and habits of stress, physical tension, and emotional reactivity even when we're not aware of them.

Here's a variation on mindful practice that is one of the most effective ways to let go of invisible tension throughout the entire body.

❊ Whole-Body Progressive Muscle Relaxation

Focus on your normal breathing, and as your attention wanders, bring it back to your breath.

Now be aware of your feet, just as they are. Imagine that you're inhaling into them. Then as you exhale, let your feet relax. Repeat this with several breaths, for half a minute or so.

Now be aware of your calves, and inhale into them. As you exhale, let your calves relax. Repeat this several times, too.

Then continue the pattern of breathing to relax, gradually moving up your body through your thighs, pelvis, lower and upper abdomen, lower and upper back, chest, shoulders, upper and lower arms, hands, neck, jaw, face, eyes, and the back and top of your head.

Then be aware of your whole body, as though it were a balloon, seeing it expand and contract as you inhale and exhale, and letting it relax as you exhale.

You can choose to focus on any or all parts of your body, stay longer with some parts, or add some as you wish.

Notice how each body part relaxes beyond the state it was in before you focused on it. At the end, notice how your whole body is more relaxed, and how you've released tension you weren't aware of.

Releasing whole-body tension

The awareness-raising and tension-releasing exercise described above, Progressive Muscle Relaxation (PMR), has been around in one version or another for a surprisingly long time, nearly one hundred years. It was created in the 1920's by a physician, Edmund Jacobson. PMR shares the same goal of releasing tension as letting the center of our breath sink – and the fact that it's been around for so long is a testimony to its effectiveness.

This version of PMR does not include Jacobson's instruction to deliberately increase tension in each body part before releasing it. That step was meant to enhance awareness of the process of releasing tension, but my own experience is that by increasing tension before we release it, we obscure awareness of the tension that already exists in that part of the body. It also doesn't seem to lead to a more relaxed state than simply relaxing the existing tension.

The benefit of a whole-body exercise, though, is clear. By deliberately focusing on many specific parts of our body, aligning them with our breathing and releasing tension in them as we exhale, we discover and let go of tension in parts of our body that we may not be aware of. As with the practice of letting the center of our breathing sink, full-body PMR often surprises us by how much tension it releases, even after we've been doing a more general mindful practice.

Adding PMR to our mindful practice enhances its effect and benefit, and doesn't require additional time. My suggestion is to start with PMR several times a week as part of the regular practice, and then include it as often as it feels right.

Summary:

By paying attention to the center of our breathing and letting it sink, we can...

- Improve our awareness of physical tension and our ability to let it go.
- Reduce habitual stress responses that feel "normal" and that we might not be aware of.

By doing a Progressive Muscle Relaxation exercise with our entire body as part of our mindful practice, we can...

- Release additional tension and patterns of stress throughout our body that we weren't aware of.
- Relieve chronically tense areas of our body.
- Enhance the benefits of mindful practice.

Chapter 3

Reduce Distractibility

If you can't meditate in a boiler room, you can't meditate.
– ALAN WATTS

Jane had retired a few years earlier from working in a department store. She was attending my class at a local senior center about mindful stress management for family caregivers of loved ones with physical or mental difficulties. Each person in the circle told why they had come, and when it was Jane's turn, she said that she'd faced an unexpected surprise – and an unpleasant one – shortly after she stopped working.

"I'd thought my husband and I would be traveling, spending time at our cottage on the lake, and visiting our grandchildren," she said. "I didn't think that he'd be diagnosed with Alzheimer's disease just a few weeks after I retired."

After we'd heard from everyone in the group, I described the basic mindful practice in this book and we practiced it for a few minutes. When I brought the group back and asked everyone how it went, she shook her head in frustration.

"I just can't make my mind quiet," she said. "I've tried meditation before, but my mind is always racing from one thing to the next and I can't stop it. I guess this just isn't for me."

You're not alone in having a mind that won't shut down, I said. Most people are easily distracted by their thoughts. Fortunately, you don't have to have a quiet mind to do this meditation. All you need to do is notice when you're distracted and shift your attention back to your breath.

"I can't even do that!" she said with frustration. "I try to remember what to do, but there are just so many things I'm worried about."

We spent more than the usual amount of time during that class on ways of staying focused on our breathing and being less distracted, and then everyone went home to practice. After a few more classes, she came in with a different story.

"I changed my mind about how much I'm distracted," she said. "I still have way too many things on my 'to do' list, but as I do what you taught us, at least I can focus on my breathing. And it's certainly making it easier to deal with my husband. I've even got him doing that t'ai chi thing you showed us when he gets agitated and worked up, and it seems to help him calm down."

There's an old joke: if you want God to laugh, make a plan. Unfortunately, the plans we make are often disrupted by life circumstances. As Jane found, not only her plans to travel with her husband after she retired were upset, but her very relationship with him was transformed by his limiting and disruptive symptoms of Alzheimer's disease. She was distressed and overwhelmed, and her difficulty concentrating made it even worse. Fortunately, her ability to focus improved with regular mindful practice, and she was able to use some distraction-reducing and calming techniques to help herself and her husband deal better with their situation.

The worst class ever

I've had more than a few of my own plans disrupted, too. The first mindful practice class I taught after I became a psychologist took place just outside of Chicago at Oak Park Hospital. It was for a group of about thirty people who'd been referred by their physicians or who were just curious about mindful practice and wanted to try it. I'd taught other meditation classes, but was still pretty excited about teaching the first one in my new professional role.

The class started at 7:00 p.m. At about 7:15, I was surprised and a bit alarmed to hear a band starting to tune up in the auditorium next to the classroom where we were meeting. By 7:30, a party for all the seventh-grade students in the Oak Park school district was in full swing. And it was loud!

My voice is not the sort that penetrates powerfully and incisively through background noise. For over sixty minutes, I shouted as loudly as I could over the music coming from next door. By the end of the class, I was hoarse and could barely speak. But early on, after a brief pause to find out what was happening, I'd made a decision not to postpone the class, or even to find another place in the hospital for us to meet. Distractions can be useful – even when they're nearly overwhelming.

Distractions as a gift

The basic mindful practice I've described says, "When you're distracted, bring your attention back to your breath." It doesn't say "*If* you're distracted..." or "*If* you're worried about remembering what you have to pick up from the grocery store on the way home..." or "*If* the clock ticking in the room seems really loud..."

The word "if" is not part of the directions for a simple reason. It is simply inevitable that we'll have distracting thoughts, hear sounds or be otherwise distracted while we're doing mindful practice. If we're dealing with a stressful situation or life challenge, inner distractions will make it all the more difficult to focus.

Mindful practice, however, allows us to do something other than be distracted: it lets us practice deliberately paying attention *despite* the distractions. As it happens, this is quite a useful life skill.

As I saw it, the incredibly noisy classroom at Oak Park Hospital during that first meditation class was an unexpected gift. As we sat focusing on our breathing and repeatedly turning attention away from the music back to our breath, many realized that, except for its volume, the music wasn't so different than many other distractions in their lives. Furthermore, it wasn't our only distraction.

Aside from the intrusion of the music itself, the people in the class also had distracting thoughts. When I asked them, I discovered that their thoughts ranged from "Why on earth don't we cancel this class and resume next week?" to "Our teacher really should have known this party was scheduled and done something about it," to "It's totally inappropriate for young seventh graders to be having a party like this!" If anything, these judgmental and emotion-laden thoughts were even more distracting than the music. The people in the class were able to practice the hard task of setting their thoughts aside, too, as well as the loud music.

I did change one thing about the class, however. Earlier than I ordinarily would have, I gave the class the exercise below (and the exercise following it as well).

❁ Move Your Fingers with Your Breath

As you do your mindful practice, let your hands rest in your lap, palms up.

Now move your fingers exactly in sync with your breathing.

As you inhale, slightly open your fingers. As you exhale, let your fingers relax.

See if paying attention to the movement of your hands helps you be less distracted.

A tool to help us focus

Our breath is a subtle thing. We don't make much of a sound when we breathe, and the physical sensation of our body rising and falling with each breath isn't easy to focus on, either. Fortunately, we don't have to pay attention to our breathing in order to stay alive (otherwise, we'd all be dead in a couple of minutes!). Although it's possible to voluntarily control how we breathe or hold our breath, normal breathing is controlled by our involuntary or autonomic nervous system. We will continue to breathe whether we're awake, asleep, driving a car or playing a video game.

Since we don't have to pay attention to our breathing, we generally don't. It's easy to be distracted from it, and it takes effort to deliberately focus on our breath. But if we add another movement to the exercise – a voluntary movement that requires more of our attention – it can help us maintain focus on our breathing.

That's what opening and closing our hands exactly in sync with our breath does. It also makes it easier to shift our attention away from what's distressing or distracting to us. The fingers don't have to move a lot, just enough so that we're aware of slightly extending and then relaxing them.

Note that we're aligning the movement of our hands with breathing, not aligning breathing with the movement of our hands. Doing the latter would manipulate our breath, and obscure the feedback about how tense we are. Because we're moving our hands in sync with our breathing, we become more aware of the naturally relaxing effect of our breath's slow rhythm.

But what if we're *really* distracted?

What if we find ourselves in an extremely distracting environment, or so mentally and emotionally preoccupied with a distressing experience that even subtly moving our fingers with our breath doesn't help us concentrate?

Rather than abandon mindful practice completely (after all, it's meant to help us when we're severely distressed), we can move our hands up and down, t'ai chi fashion, in sync with our breathing, as in the exercise below. This "intervention level" of the exercise can help cut through more significant distractions and make it easier to relax. I have done this with people who are very anxious or having a panic attack, older people with dementia, and many others having a hard time concentrating. When I was in my early 20's, I needed to concentrate on slow t'ai chi movements, too, before I could meditate successfully. Moving our hands slowly and paying attention to their movement is often an effective way to quiet a particularly anxious state of mind.

❋ Move Your Arms and Hands as You Breathe

Keeping your hands in sync with your breathing, make their movements bigger, as if you were doing t'ai chi.

Palms up, let your hands rise a foot or so as you inhale, then turn your hands over and let them sink back as you exhale.

Continue to let your hands follow your breath. Notice if this movement helps you stay focused on your breathing.

We may be reluctant to do this, however, if we're around other people and feel shy about conspicuously moving our hands up and down. The next exercise is less obvious, and worth trying when we're really distraught or distracted in a public place. This also works really well as an intervention to help others calm down when they're upset. I've used it with medical patients in the hospital and with my own family members.

One of the signs that we're relaxed is that we experience the center of our breathing in the lower part of our abdomen. Placing a hand over the lower part of our belly and imagining breathing in and out of the palm is another "intervention level" exercise we can do to relax when we're really distracted or distressed. Naturally and without forcing, it guides us to breathe more slowly and deeply, gently leading us into what is called "diaphragmatic breathing." It also takes our mind off distressing thoughts.

❋ Breathe Through the Palm of Your Hand

Place your hand over the lower part of your belly.

Imagine that you're breathing in and out of the palm of your hand.

Notice what happens to your breathing, and to the level of distress and distraction you're experiencing.

Although breathing through the palm of our hand is particularly useful when we're in a public situation, we can take the "stealth" aspects of it even further. If we feel self-conscious about moving a hand to our belly, we can simply imagine a hand in that position and breathe into it. Or we can imagine breathing in and out of our belly button.

This version of the exercise is also helpful when it may be physically difficult to move our hands. I have done this with hospital patients in an Intensive Care Unit who were on a respirator to help their breathing, or who had IV lines in their arms that made it difficult for them to move *anything*. They told me it was very empowering for them to breathe in and out of their belly button and feel they could make themselves more relaxed and comfortable in such a situation.

With my children, it's also been very helpful to have them place a hand over their belly and breathe into it when they've been anxious about taking a trip, going to school, or anything else. It's been especially effective when they can't quiet down before bedtime – which I suspect most parents will find useful!

Some FMC on distractions

Here are some frequently made comments I often hear from people just starting mindful practice who are distressed by being distracted.

I can't find a quiet, undistracted place to practice.

We don't need a quiet place to do mindful practice! In fact, since the goal is to help us be more relaxed and peaceful around the difficulties of daily life, it's probably better that we practice where it isn't perfectly quiet or serene. In fact, if we want to change our response to a particular place or time in our daily life that is disruptive, distressing or distracting, we should try to do mindful practice in that environment.

I can't quiet my mind, so I guess mindful practice isn't for me.

We all get distracted by thoughts and feelings. What mindful practice does is give us something to do with those internal distractions, as well as the external ones. In fact, as we practice shifting our attention away from distractions, we'll get better at it. Eventually, we'll find ourselves less distracted by what's going on inside us and around us, and better able to focus on what we care about. A quiet mind (or at least a *quieter* mind) is the result of mindful practice, not a requirement to start.

If I'm distracted, I'm not really being mindful – right?

Some forms of meditation or mindful practice aspire to bring us to a state of mind free from distractions, but not this one. The goal here is to learn to notice distractions and respond to them differently. In fact, distractions are a good thing: we wouldn't learn as much about shifting attention away from distractions if we didn't have distractions to practice with. So whenever we notice we're distracted and shift our attention to our breath, we're doing the mindful practice just fine.

The Benefits of Distraction

There are great benefits to learning the skill of shifting attention away from distractions in our daily life. Here's the best example I know.

When researchers study the effects of mindful practice on people who have chronic pain, they find several things. First, there's a small to moderate improvement in the intensity of a person's pain, how often they experience pain, and the length of a pain episode. There's a bigger improvement, however, in how much their activities are impaired by pain. Mindful practice significantly reduces how much chronic pain keeps people from doing the things they really want to do.

This makes perfect sense, when we think about it. When we do mindful practice, we shift our attention away from distractions and back to our breathing. Maybe we have to do it as many as five or even ten times in a minute – and anything we do that often, we get good at!

Shifting our attention to where we want it during mindful practice becomes a skill we get better at, and more importantly, a skill we can use for other purposes. Someone with chronic pain learns to shift attention away from what they don't want to be distracted by (pain) and focus on things they do want to give their attention to (their work, a hobby, a conversation, reading, playing with a grandchild, and so on). The result can be less impairment from pain and greater enjoyment of life. For any of us, it can mean a significant improvement in our quality of life if we find relief from chronic stress, intrusive thoughts, emotional distress or physical discomfort.

So after we've practiced for a while, our ability to shift attention away from distress or discomfort and back to things that are important is likely to improve. That's what Eleanor, the woman with the annoying neighbors, found in the introductory story to this book. Like her, we may find that developing the ability to keep our attention where we want it may be one of the most important and life-changing benefits of mindful practice.

Summary

By letting our hands open and close gently in sync with our breathing, we can...

- More easily set aside distractions.
- Reinforce the quieting effect of the slow rhythm of our breathing.

By moving our hands up and down in a motion similar to t'ai chi, we can...

- Cut through more severe distractions and distress.
- Find a greater level of whole-body relaxation.

By putting our hand on our lower belly and imagining that we're breathing through the palm of our hand (or by imagining we're breathing through our belly button), we can...

- Cut through severe distractions in a more private way.

Chapter 4

Practice Everywhere

Everywhere I go, I still have time to meditate. People think meditating is sitting there, nobody bothering you, but you can even talk and still meditate.

– JET LI

Joe was another preventive cardiology patient who came to see me. He had some difficulty remembering to take his medications, and also found himself becoming more irritated with little things in his life – which surprised him, because he had recently retired. After nearly fifty years of work, he now had a lot of free time on his hands, and he didn't seem to know what to do with himself except play golf with his friends.

"I'm not even enjoying my golf anymore," he said. "I go out with my friends a few times a week, and it's so frustrating – I'll hit a bad shot and get angry with the game, with myself, with everything. The guy who said, 'Golf is a good walk spoiled,' got it exactly right."

He also found himself hovering over his wife in the kitchen and around the house, and getting on her nerves. "She doesn't seem to want my advice about anything," he said. "I know, I know – she's *been doing things her way for decades, and she doesn't need me to mess with her routine. But when I see her doing something that could be done better, it's hard to keep my mouth shut."*

He was open to trying mindful practice, if only to add something to his routine. But after a month or so, he began to get excited about it. "You know, I think I figured out why I was following my wife around. I didn't have anything to do, and it just felt good being near her. But with this new thing you have me doing, I don't feel the pressure to comment on how she does things. I'll just read the paper or something, and let her do what she does."

He also added additional practice sessions to his meditation routine. "I started out once a day, like you said. But after a couple of weeks, I began to see big changes happening, and I thought, if once a day is good, how about doing it three or four times a day, even if it's just a few minutes here and there, wherever I happen to be? So that's what I'm doing now, and it's really great."

What he liked best about it, though, was a total surprise to him. "The best part is that now I can enjoy my golf game again. I still hit bad shots – but I'm able to remember that it's a beautiful day, and I'm out with my friends. When I walk up to the next shot, I'm in a better mood, and instead of blowing that one, too, it's more likely to be a good shot. I've even taken a few strokes off my handicap!"

Change isn't easy to handle. Even when it's something we look forward to, such as retirement, a better job, moving to a different place, or the arrival of a new family member, change can be stressful and upset our routine in difficult ways. Joe found that retirement confronted him with a set of problems he didn't anticipate, which affected his relationship with his wife and his enjoyment of activities he had found interesting and fun. But by doing mindful practice at different times and in different places during the day, he was able to generalize the effects of mindful practice more quickly into his life and find new and better ways to appreciate the changes he was dealing with after retirement.

❋ Practice at Different Times and Places

Do your basic ten-minute mindful practice every day. Be as consistent as you can.

As you are able, though, occasionally do your daily basic practice (sometimes with whole-body PMR) at different times and in different places.

Do it in locations where you're stressed – and places where you're not stressed as well.

Different times, different places

It's often easiest to do mindful practice in the same place, at the same time every day. Perhaps it's most convenient to fit it in to our routine first thing in the morning, or right after we get to work before there's much going on. Or maybe we think of it as a way of decompressing right after we get home from work, or fit it in before bedtime as a way of relaxing and getting ready to sleep.

Something like that works well for almost everyone, including me, and doing a regular mindful practice routine in the same place at the same time every day offers significant benefits. If we reach the low end of our "range of tension" at least once a day and stay there for several minutes, we're expanding our capacity to be less reactive to stressors and more mindful of how to deal with them.

As positive, convenient and effective as that routine may be, however, there's one element missing: it doesn't *generalize* the effects of our mindful practice to other situations throughout the day as effectively as it could. I sometimes tell people, "If the only time you were stressed was at 5:30 p.m. while you were sitting in a comfortable chair in your living room, that would be the only time and place you'd need to practice."

In fact, sitting in a favorite chair when the day is winding down would probably be one of the *least* stressful moments of the day. While it would be a great time and place to decompress, it wouldn't be the best place to directly tackle the stress and tension experienced during the day.

In contrast, what would happen if we did mindful practice at the times and in the places where we're *most* stressed, at least some of the time? Even more challenging, what might happen if we practiced at the times and in the places that have conditioned us to become stressed even if we just think about them (like the example of students thinking about an assignment or an exam)?

Things commonly associated with chronic stress might be our desk at work, a person we don't like very much, situations when we have to juggle many different tasks, or when a lot is riding on being our very best. Look for places and times at work associated with stress, at home in rooms that have a burdensome "to do" list associated with them, or even sitting in the car in a parking lot. Then take a few minutes to do our mindful practice in those situations and let go of some of the reactivity associated with them.

Healing painful memories

For most of us, though, situations we experience in the present are only a small part of what distresses us. We often have memories of past events that haunt us and may keep us from feeling good about ourselves or doing the things we want to do with our life. Can mindful practice help change those memories – or at least our reaction to them?

To some degree, it can. As it does with our conditioned responses, mindful practice can defuse the intensity of difficult memories and create a broader context for past experiences that make them easier to live with. As we mentally call forth a difficult situation or person, we can be mindfully aware of the tension and distress that arises from that memory. Then as we exhale, we can release part of it. In the treatment of PTSD and other anxiety disorders, this is a version of *exposure therapy* and *response prevention* – and over time, this practice can defuse at least some of our triggered responses as we recall distressing situations or people.

For instance, suppose we've had a negative experience with a particular person. We might relax into our mindful practice and then bring that person to mind, noticing our physical, emotional and mental responses, and then breathe into those reactions to release them. Over time, continued work in this way can help us ease some of the tension and reactivity we have around that person, and perhaps also help us see that person in a different way. We may come to see that what they did to hurt us was less deliberate and more out of ignorance, or that our life was not as badly impaired by their action as we may have thought. Or we may have some other insight about that person or ourselves. Mindfully working with our experience of them and our perspective on what they did can allow us to let go of some of our distress and see them and ourselves more clearly. It may allow us to directly address the problem we have with them or move on from it.

If we're thinking about using mindful practice to change deep experiences of abuse or trauma from the past, however, it's a good idea to do so while seeing an experienced psychologist or counselor. Mindful practice alone may not be appropriate or sufficient to address what we experienced, and a professional therapist can bring other counseling and therapeutic techniques to bear on the situation we're dealing with. As I said earlier, even if we can't change what happened in the past, we can often change how much it affects us now – and doing so may make it possible to reclaim the life we truly want to live.

Mindful physical exercise

Joggers all move in different ways. Some run in a very relaxed and fluid style, and some have very constrained movements, at times so stiff that their arms barely move and their shoulders are tucked into their ears.

We tend to forget that we're tense and stressed not only when we're sitting down. If we want to truly generalize the benefits of mindful practice into everything we do, we need to practice not only when we're sitting in different locations and at different times, but when our body is standing, walking, running, exercising and doing other things.

❈ Mindful Walking and Exercise

Include your mindful practice in any rhythmic exercise you do (such as walking, running, bicycling, using a treadmill or elliptical trainer, and so on).

If you're walking, for example, pay attention to the pace of your walk and the slower rhythm of your breath. Let them relate to each other in whatever way seems natural, without forcing.

Keep your eyes open, and your attention on the ground about ten to fifteen feet in front of you.

As with the sitting practice, when you're distracted, bring your attention back to your breath.

You can also do mindful practice during a quiet exercise such as yoga or stretching. During an exercise such as yoga, pay attention to your breath and to how your body feels as you do the exercise. When does it feel right to inhale, and when to exhale? Again, as you find yourself distracted, return attention to your breath.

The good news is that the version of mindful practice above doesn't take any additional time out of our schedule, because we fold it into the movement and exercise that we're already doing. The other good news is that it will help us exercise better and more efficiently, because when we're relaxed, we're not tensed up in ways that interfere with our movement. It also will help us play competitive sports with more focus and less tension, which as Joe found, can often improve our performance.

In fact, walking mindfully is the best way I know to clear my head when I find my mind cluttered and distracted. My office used to be on the third floor of the Appleton Heart Institute. When I was feeling a bit overwhelmed, in good weather I would go outside and mindfully circle the hospital. When it was raining or cold, I would walk through the halls of the hospital doing my mindful practice. In less than ten minutes, I would be back in my office with my head clear, ready for what I needed to do next.

Based on that positive experience, I suggested to the doctors and nurses I worked with that they do this as they walk from one patient room to the next, or from one hospital unit to another. Folding even a minute or two of this mindful walking exercise into our daily activities is an easy way to hit the reset button so we can be fresh and clear-headed for whatever's next.

One or two breaths, everywhere

By far the easiest way to generalize the benefits is to do brief versions of our mindful practice – just one or two mindful breaths – in many different situations throughout the day. We need to remember to do it, and it requires attention, but it doesn't take any additional time out of our routine.

❅ Practice Everywhere

Throughout the day, take one or two mindful breaths in a variety of situations. Move your attention to your breath, and relax as you exhale.

Try doing this when you're waiting for a traffic light to change, before you get out of your car to go shopping, while you're waiting in line, or during television commercials. Think of other times to do it, as well.

In fact, take a moment to practice right now.

Why does taking just one or two mindful breaths throughout the day make a difference?

When we take even a single breath with awareness, the deeper state of relaxation that we evoke counteracts the conscious and unconscious stresses that we're experiencing at that particular moment. We're breaking the habit of being stressed by the situation we're in or by the thoughts we're having, even if we're not aware of that stress.

As we'll see in the next chapter, mindful practice not only can release tension in specific situations, but can give us the opportunity to consciously choose how we react to difficulties and stressors throughout the day.

Summary

By doing our basic ten-minute mindful practice at different times and places, we can...

- More easily set aside distractions and reduce reactivity in different situations.
- Reinforce the quieting effect of the slow rhythm of our breathing throughout the day.

By doing mindful practice while walking or exercising, we can...

- Effectively clear our head from distractions.
- Reduce stress associated with physical activity.
- Do mindful practice without taking additional time out of our day.

By taking a breath or two mindfully throughout the day to relax, we can...

- Break unconscious patterns of stress and tension associated with a wide variety of situations (driving, at work, at home, etc.) in which we can't do a ten-minute practice.
- Generalize the benefits of mindful practice into every part of our life.

Chapter 5

Make Mindful Choices

Meditation is the ultimate mobile device; you can use it anywhere, anytime, unobtrusively.

– SHARON SALZBERG

Dr. Beth was a successful and respected physician, but she was tormented by the thought that she might have been responsible for the death of one of her patients. The patient had come to her office with diffuse symptoms and discomfort, and she'd sent him home with advice to see how things developed and call if they got worse. Two days later the patient was in the emergency room. Shortly after that, he died of a rare and hard-to-identify infection.

Dr. Beth had been in practice for twenty years, and was highly regarded by her colleagues. She was proud of doing good work for her patients, and tried to be what she privately called a "Super Doc." She didn't want to be anything less than the best. But she was being called in front of the hospital's Care Review Board to discuss her treatment of the patient, and she was plagued with self-doubt and guilt. "What did I miss?" she agonized. "I've gone over my notes and my memory of the exam, and I can't see how I would have done anything other than what I did. Maybe I'm just not a very good physician."

Her colleagues were supportive. Two of them had informally reviewed the case and told her there was nothing she could – or should – have done differently. The other senior members of her practice reminded her that perfection in medical practice is impossible. Sometimes we do our best and things just don't work out, they told her. She appreciated their support, but couldn't see how she could continue to practice medicine while feeling such intense internal self-doubt and stress. "I've started to second-guess myself, and I've consulted with my partners on routine patients that I don't need to consult on. I can't go on working like this."

She was willing to start a mindful practice that would help her set aside self-doubt and anxiety and focus her attention positively on the emotional and medical needs of her patients. After a few weeks of regular practice at her office and at home, she felt calmer. "I'm at least starting to sleep better," she said. "And I've stopped consulting with my colleagues about patients that are straightforward. But I'm still worried about the Care Review Board."

We talked about how she could use her mindful practice to stay factual and composed in her presentation to the Board, yet also share some of her feelings about the patient dying.

She came for one last visit the day after she met with the Care Review Board. "It went better than I thought it would," she said. "I could talk about what I felt but didn't break down, and I was able to answer their questions pretty well. The people on the Board were actually much more understanding than I thought they would be."

She looked at me seriously. "If it hadn't gone well, I was considering giving up my career as a physician. I think mindful practice has helped me see things in a better perspective."

So maybe you don't need to be 'Super Doc' anymore, I suggested.

"Oh, I'm not so sure about that," she smiled. "But 'Super Doc' doesn't have to be 'Perfect Doc' any more, and that's a big relief."

Making a mistake that costs someone their life is a terrible experience. The guilt and shame from making such an error, the loss of self-confidence, the discouragement and doubt can all be crippling to our sense of self-worth and ability to function. I had a psychotherapy client who killed someone while drinking and driving and felt so guilty that he chose never to drive a vehicle again. I have counseled people who became disabled due to their own foolish behavior and wanted to end their lives because their body no longer looked or functioned the way it did before. I've also worked with smokers who developed lung cancer and felt enormously guilty for putting their family through the trauma of their diagnosis and treatment, and in a number of cases, their dying and death.

As difficult as these situations were, and as understandable as their extreme response was, there were other paths these people could have taken if they'd had the assistance of mindful practice. But I'm not talking just about being more relaxed or reducing stress. In the face of such a life-defining event, being mindful means not only lowering stress, but making a choice about the attitude we take toward what happened, our understanding of our role in it, and about what comes next.

Dr. Beth was not actually responsible for the death of her patient. But she believed she might have been, which deeply distressed her and eroded her self-confidence. Fortunately, mindful practice allowed her to moderate the intensity of her reactions. Just as importantly, she was able to use it to address the anxiety and lack of confidence she experienced in her daily practice and the fear that overwhelmed her at the prospect of meeting with the Care Review Board.

In addition to engaging in the simple mindful practice several times a day, here's what she did.

❋ Take Two Mindful Breaths

Throughout your day, notice when you're stressed or upset. At those times, shift your attention to your next two breaths.

During the first breath, as you inhale, pull your attention away from the difficult situation and be aware of your breath. As you exhale, let yourself relax.

During the second breath, as you inhale, think of a word that represents something positive you'd like to bring to that moment. The word might be "peace," "love," "compassion," "calm," "curious," "grateful," or whatever feels right to you.

As you exhale, say that word or phrase silently to yourself to evoke the feeling and experience you want to bring to the situation. Be aware of how your experience changes.

Now, holding that intention, go forward.

Relax and focus with two mindful breaths

One of my medical friends, a pediatrician, pauses for a moment before entering an exam room to see one of his patients. He knows that behind that door is a young person who may be scared and a parent who may be worried. What he does next, he knows, will make a difference in their lives.

"So I pause for a moment before I open the door," he told me. "I take a breath, and I remember how grateful I am to be able to do this work and care for young people and families."

Isn't he the sort of doctor we all wish we had – and the sort of person we'd like to be as we open the doors that challenge us in our life?

After doing the daily practice and generalization exercises for several weeks, Dr. Beth slowly regained her confidence with her patients by taking two mindful breaths before she entered an exam room. The first breath helped her set aside anxiety and self-doubt. The second helped her focus on being compassionate with her patient's feelings and medical needs. She also took two mindful breaths before she entered her meeting with the Care Review Board, as well as several times during that meeting. This helped her reduce her anxiety and see the Board members as people who cared about her as well as about what happened to her patient.

Note that taking two mindful breaths works far better when we've been doing a daily ten-minute practice for a while. Regular practice cultivates the association of our exhaled breath with being relaxed. This makes taking the first breath all the more effective at helping us release tension in a difficult situation. Infusing the second breath with a positive intention can then lead us to a better response and outcome than simply letting our feelings and thoughts run away with us.

This is not to say that it's easy to be calm and focused in every situation. It's just *easier* – and in many situations, even difficult ones, it becomes a choice we can make. But sometimes it may be impossible to be intentional about our reactions: on hearing of the death of a loved one, discovering we have a serious medical problem, or during other painful life-changing experiences. When we're caught up in a powerful moment, we need to let ourselves fully react to it. That's part of being human, too. Mindful practice can then help us regain our balance when we're ready to do that.

As difficult as this may seem, many professionals and ordinary people learn how to become relaxed, aware and effective in crises. Emergency medical technicians, physicians, nurses, police officers, fire fighters, airline pilots, and others handle daily situations that would throw most of us into a panic. They usually learn to do this during their training and in the early years of their work by what amounts to a variation on our mindful practice. By being exposed to a wide range of dangerous, stressful and emotional situations and doing their job safely and effectively in those conditions, they practice being calm and focused under stress. They may not specifically learn to take two breaths – but it would help any of them to add this practice to their repertoire.

The rest of us can learn to do it, too, and we'll have plenty of occasions to use it. Imagine, for instance, being on the phone with someone. It's not an easy conversation, and we're getting wound up, angry or frustrated. Instead of responding out of those feelings, we can take a mindful breath and let go of some of our tension. We can then another breath to focus on a positive quality such as patience, kindness or simple curiosity (why does the person we're talking with feel that way?) that we want to bring into the conversation.

We can also take two mindful breaths in a face-to-face conversation or argument. We can do it with our children – or our parents. Or we can take two mindful breaths to relax and focus as we get up to make a presentation in front of a group of people, when we're driving in heavy traffic or a rainstorm, before we go in for a stressful meeting or interview, or in the middle of something important that requires our best. As we consciously choose to calm ourselves and bring peace, love, patience or other positive qualities into difficult situations, we bring our highest values into our greatest challenges.

Summary

By mindfully taking two breaths in difficult situations and with people who are challenging to us, we can...

- Reduce the tension of the moment.
- Set aside negative thoughts and feelings.
- Act on our most positive intention in that situation.
- Start to actively create experiences that reflect our highest values.

Chapter 6

Toward a Mindful Life

God, grant me the serenity to accept the things
  I cannot change,
the courage to change the things I can,
and the wisdom to know the difference.

— REINHOLD NIEBUHR

When I was in my early twenties, I bought a house with a friend. I didn't have enough income from my part-time job to even afford a car, but my friend (who was working full-time) and I found ourselves in a unique set of circumstances where it became possible to purchase a house cheaply from someone who needed to sell it fast. My parents helped with a small down payment and by co-signing the loan, and to our surprise, there we were: homeowners.

It was a small older house in a low-income neighborhood, and it needed a lot of work. But it had character and a back yard with a mulberry tree. I painted the outside, my friend's father did some repair work, and we settled in.

Then one afternoon, we came home to find that the house had been broken into and we'd been robbed. Clothes were strewn around the bedrooms, our cheap television set and stereo were gone, and even a few pans were missing from the kitchen. The back door was broken where the thieves had pried it open. We didn't lose much of value (or have much to lose), but we felt shocked, violated, hurt. We didn't know how to react or what to do.

So I took half a dozen six-inch spikes and nailed the back door shut. There aren't many things I've done in my life that felt better and seemed to make more sense than driving nails through that door into the door frame. *That was where the thieves came through*, I thought to myself, *and no one was coming through that door again if I had anything to say about it.*

The back door stayed nailed shut for nearly a year. During the first few months, whenever I was in the house I was acutely aware of the back door and what had happened. Then I gradually stopped thinking about it, and just accepted that a nailed-shut back door was a natural part of life.

It wasn't until I finally realized that what I'd done was hurting my very patient friend and myself far more than it was protecting us that I was able to do something different.

As I pulled the nails out of the door, I thought about how overwhelmed and angry I'd felt when I drove them in. If I'd been thinking even a little more calmly and clearly, I knew that I'd have found a better way to prevent another break-in that still allowed us to use our back door: a more secure lock!

In my twenties, I didn't have much insight or many inner resources. At the time I nailed that door shut, I was beginning to change what I didn't like about my life but still didn't understand how my reactive feelings and thoughts were limiting me. Today, though, I find a gift in my overwrought reaction to the break-in. As I go through my life now, I often ask myself if I've nailed something shut, often without realizing it, that should have stayed open.

Thankfully, the inner work I was doing back then – mainly t'ai chi and a beginning meditation practice – eventually made it possible for me to take the nails out of the door and go on with my life. Those two activities helped me calm my fear and think clearly about the situation. Still, it took a long time to get beyond my initial reaction to gain perspective and see that there was an effective way to secure the door that would keep my friend and I safe and also give us access to our back yard.

When we react strongly to situations, it's often because we feel threatened or hurt and we experience the defensive urge to "fight, take flight, or freeze in place." Or it may be that our protective instincts are aroused when we see others being threatened or hurt. Real threats need to be acted upon, but our feelings of anxiety, fear and anger are not always about the situation in front of us. I wasn't self-aware enough, and didn't have enough perspective after the break-in, to see that the danger had passed and that I could respond to the situation differently and more effectively.

Significant parts of our lives are spent at the mercy of unconscious reactions that have very little to do with the truth of the situation we're in. Many of the reasons for our fears and anxieties (including the impulse to nail a door shut) are hidden from us, and we assume those responses are simply a natural reaction that anyone would have. That often simply isn't true. We may avoid a person at work because they remind us of someone who bullied us in school, but a friend, not conditioned by our personal history, may get along fine with him or her. Or we may be the only person in our family afraid of flying, simply because we experienced three minutes of turbulent flight twenty years ago.

Our conditioned responses often don't fit reality. Even the bumps and bruises of normal daily life – from working under a deadline, to not having much control over our work, to normal conflicts with co-workers and family, to ordinary worries about money, to uncertainties about minor health problems – can trigger an over-reaction of being anxious and fearful, overwhelmed and discouraged. Often this is because of the toxic assumptions, negative thoughts, expectations and past experiences we've come to associate with those issues.

It can be worse, though, when we encounter a major life difficulty such as a significant medical problem, a major financial or legal threat, the loss of a loved one, or a powerful event that turns our world upside down. These are challenging enough in themselves, but they may also evoke an even stronger conditioned response – perhaps numbness, rage, fear, or an overwhelming desire to nail a door shut – that's about something other than the situation we're actually facing.

But with regular mindful practice and an intentional first breath, we can defuse or diminish some of those conditioned reactions as well as reduce the intensity of the situation itself. A purposeful second breath to set a positive direction can then lead us to a simpler, better, and more effective response to our difficulties. Mindful practice frees us to be more genuine, appropriate and intentional in responding to what's happening to us right now.

Even so, we won't always be able to have peaceful, enlightened reactions to what we encounter in life. We'll still sometimes feel angry, disappointed, or hurt. When that happens, though, we're less likely to get lost in our fear and pain, and less likely to feel helpless and powerless about dealing with our situation. What mindful practice does when we encounter life's challenges and conflicts is make it easier to respond to them authentically and fully with our whole self.

Living our truth

It matters a lot how we think about the difficult things that happen to us, how we believe they've changed us, and how we see ourselves in relationship to those situations. Many worthwhile books and counselors offer ways of maintaining hope, suggesting that we focus on the good in life and develop a positive attitude, no matter what limitations or losses we may be facing. But just saying, "I'm going to change how I think about this terrible thing that's happened to me" – particularly when we've lost a loved one or have serious, persistent problems that aren't going away – may seem more like trying to convince ourselves of a lie than really changing things.

My own experience and that of many people I've worked with leads me to believe that it's more effective to do mindful practice *before* we try to consciously change how we think about and respond to life's challenges. Our ways of thinking, feeling and seeing are often unconsciously conditioned, and we need to become less reactive overall and more aware of our conditioned responses before we can make an intentional change in how we think and feel about something. When we do that preparatory mindful work, however, new doors open. We can begin to choose the way we genuinely want to be, and follow the path that feels most real, true and meaningful to us.

Here are some of the ways of being that become easier after developing a regular mindful practice.

Being patient

Impatience is all about expectations. Our expectations about how we think things ought to be can make even ordinary experiences emotionally difficult, such as waiting in line or being caught in traffic. Mindful practice helps us calm our impatience and reduce the inner pressure of the expectations we place on ourselves, other people, and the world. As we lower our emotional reactivity and our attachment to our expectations, it becomes easier to deal patiently with the world as it is.

Accepting things as they are

Some of us try to deny the seriousness of the difficulties that life brings our way, or go the opposite direction and get caught up in frustrated and discouraged thoughts about our problems. Mindful practice makes it easier to see and accept the way things are, and whether they can or can't be changed. However, acceptance doesn't mean that our difficulties don't matter or that we shouldn't have thoughts and feelings about them. Mindful acceptance is simply a way to see our circumstances and our experience more clearly, as they are. In doing so, we no longer let our perceptions be ruled by wishful thinking, reactive thoughts, hurt feelings or pain. Mindful acceptance lets us more clearly see ourselves, our thoughts and feelings, other people, and the situation we're in – and then discern what is truly ours to do next.

Being kind to others and ourselves

Once we see ourselves, others and the world more clearly, mindful practice gives us the opportunity to choose, at least in part, how to respond to our difficulties. The choice to be kind to ourselves and others is a path of surprising strength, a way of becoming caring and compassionate, yet resilient. Being kind also makes it easier to acknowledge our common humanity with everyone who has problems – that is, all of us! We may even see the wisdom of letting others be kind to us, and ask for professional help or talk with a friend about what we're going through.

Keeping things in perspective

Regular mindful practice helps us be patient, accept and see clearly the situation we're in, and be kind to other people and ourselves. It accomplishes those remarkable feats in large part by giving us practice in keeping our emotions and thoughts in a healthy and realistic perspective, making them neither too large nor too small. Over time, mindful practice lets our mental, emotional and physical reactivity evolve, change and heal, gently and naturally as we open ourselves to the broad range of our human experience. As we do, we become more aware of what's most true and important to us. No matter how far things are from the way we'd like them to be – and how deeply we find ourselves mired in "the tragic gap" that Parker Palmer talks about between the way things are and the way we want them to be – mindful practice gives us a better chance of staying centered in what we care about genuinely, creatively and with a whole heart.

Courage and serenity

One of the greatest life challenges is to discern what we can change and what we can't, and to respond appropriately to each. As the Serenity Prayer so eloquently states, we need to cultivate courage to change the things we can change and inner serenity to accept the things we can't, as well as wisdom to know the difference between them. Mindful practice helps us be serene, courageous and wise, as we need to be.

Whether our personal or circumstantial difficulties can be changed or not, mindful practice can keep us from losing ourselves in fear, anxiety or pain. As we see our challenges more clearly and respond genuinely to them, we may discover a way to live whole-heartedly even with a serious life problem such as a medical issue, a loss, or a personal crisis. We may also find ourselves more loving, compassionate, and committed to the activities and people we care about. This is the door that mindful practice opens for us: the clear-headed freedom to respond to what life brings us in a way that is true to who we are and how we want to be.

Whatever challenges you face, may you be safe, may you be well, may you find peace.

> *All you need to know is that the future is wide open*
> *and you are about to create it by what you do.*
>
> — PEMA CHÖDRÖN

Gratitude

The simple mindful practice described here has been a central part of my life, and I am immensely grateful to the wise and insightful teachers who've taught and helped me along the way. I particularly want to thank Crystal, who patiently taught my tense, anxious twenty-something self a graceful Wu style of t'ai chi, and my friend Dr. Jerry Epps, who taught me to meditate from a perspective embracing many traditions and who has been my mentor and spiritual brother for almost forty years. I'd also like to thank Parker Palmer and the Center for Courage & Renewal for offering me the opportunity to become a Circle of Trust facilitator, as well as the profound insight about what it is to stand in the tragic gap between the way things are and what is possible – and to hold that tension in life-giving ways.

I also want to acknowledge the remarkable people whose writing and work on mindful practice that I've been inspired by. I particularly want to lift up the late Stephen Levine for his lyrical yet deeply personal and grounded understanding of life, death and meditation. His book, *A Gradual Awakening* (Anchor Books, 1979), profoundly changed my life many years ago. This eloquent, poetic and insightful work focuses more on mindful practice in general than mindfulness-based practices to help manage stress or achieve other goals, but at a time when there are so many goal-oriented books about mindfulness (including this one), it is a refreshing change of pace.

I'd also like to thank Dr. Herbert Benson at Harvard for his groundbreaking research and creation of a meditation practice that could be used by medical patients and others who are not part of a religious tradition. One of the first western researchers to scientifically study meditation, Dr. Benson developed and researched a non-religious secular meditation practice that he called "the relaxation response." He was an extraordinary pioneer in making meditation an acceptable practice in western academia and the medical world. It is hard to imagine mindful practice being accepted to the extent it has been without Dr. Benson's pioneering efforts.

There are so many others whom I am grateful for as well, including Jack Kornfield for his insights about daily life "after the ecstasy" of enlightenment, Sharon Salzberg for her deep commitment to being genuine and holding others with lovingkindness, Richard Moss for his focus on practicing aliveness, Jon Kabat-Zinn for making mindful practice the profoundly supportive tool that it has become for medical patients, and the list goes on. So many insights, so many gifts.

There are also many people who helped with the practical aspects of creating this book. My friends, family and colleagues who offered their reactions and critiques to the manuscript have helped it to become far better than it was initially. Many thanks also to my copy editor, Jane Salisbury, who not only made the text more concise and focused, but led me to a more mindful awareness of my habits and peculiarities as a writer.

Finally, I'd like to thank my amazing wife, Laurin, and our equally amazing daughters, Katie and Kara, for their love and support. I love you, family! You give me my most important reason to practice being my best mindful self every day.

Notes, Comments and References

Introduction: Living in the Tragic Gap

Page xiii. Parker Palmer's thoughts about living in the "tragic gap" are online at http://www.couragerenewal.org/the-tragic-gap/ and in his book, *Healing the Heart of Democracy: The Courage to Create a Politics Worthy of the Human Spirit* (2011, Jossy-Bass).

Page xv. Psychologist Dr. Kristen Neff has done excellent research on *self-compassion*, showing that being kind to ourselves, seeing our common humanity with others, and being mindful of our feelings and experience leads to greater resilience and improved coping with difficulties for adolescents, adults and seniors. She has thoughtfully made her research papers available at http://self-compassion.org/the-research/

Chapter 1: A Simple Mindful Practice

Page 1. For the sake of convenience and brevity, throughout this book I refer to the exercises and activities as "mindful practice." In academic and other writing about mindfulness, they would likely be called "mindfulness-based practices" because they cultivate mindfulness as a means to an end other than spiritual insight and growth, having the explicit objective of helping people reduce stress, cope with life better, and obtain other positive benefits (e.g., Jon Kabat-Zinn's "Mindfulness-Based Stress Reduction"). I respect that traditional academic way of naming the process, but gently set it aside as needlessly cumbersome.

Page 3. I recently decided to check if whether what I've been saying for years about the number of types of meditation being comparable to the number of medications was actually true. What I found in the journal *Drug Discovery Today* (August, 2014) was that, since the time it started in 1827 until 2013, the United States Food and Drug Administration has approved 1,453 drugs, and adds thirty or so more per year to that list. Considering that each type of meditation has several different parts (what we do, what we pay attention to, etc.) and that each part can be done in different ways (hundreds of different mantras can be used, for instance), I'd guess that 1500 vastly underestimates the types of meditation out there. On the other hand, there are multiple ways to deliver medications (by pill, liquid, intravenously, etc.), various doses, and many ways to combine different medications in a single delivery system. Call it a draw.

Page 4. Repetition and the gentle rhythm of the breath has been an important part of many meditation practices for hundreds of years and leads to physical relaxation and quieting of the mind, as was outlined by Dr. Herbert Benson.

- Benson, H. (1975). *The Relaxation Response,* chap. 5. New York: William Morrow.

Page 6. Is mindful practice or meditation really a different and better way to relax than, say, reading a book or going for a walk?

I believe that any serious look beyond short-term superficial symptom relief reveals that yes, it is – and to a surprising extent. For instance, even early researchers (Benson, 1975) noted a change in brain wave functioning, with proportionately greater alpha rhythm patterns associated with meditation than during normal relaxing activities. They also found startlingly lower oxygen metabolism occurring within a few minutes of starting meditation – an astonishing physiological change that is usually only achieved at that magnitude after hours of sleep. There are other physiological effects as well, such as the changes in HRV discussed in the text and lowered physiological arousal. For example:

- Yackel, K., Schwarz, L.A., Kam, K., et al. (2017). Breathing control center neurons that promote arousal in mice. *Science, 355,* 1411–1524

So there really is something different happening to our body and our brain when we do a breath-focused mindful practice, as well as when we look at the ongoing and long-term benefits, which is what this book you're reading mostly focuses on. Furthermore, mindful practice offers benefits far beyond those of ordinary activities to our psychological health and our physical health.

- Keng, S.L., Smoski, M.J. & Robins, C.J. (2011). Effects of mindfulness on psychological health: a review of empirical studies. *Clinical Psychology Review, (31(6),* 1041–1056.
- Gotink, R.A., Chu, P., Busschbach, J.J.V., Benson, H., Fricchione, G.L., Hunink, M. (2015). Standardised mindfulness-based interventions in healthcare: an overview of systematic reviews and meta-analyses of RCTs. *Public Library of Science (PLOS ONE),* https://doi.org/10.1371/journal.pone.0124344.

Page 10. 16 waking hours per day = 960 minutes. Practicing ten minutes per day takes about one percent of the time we're awake.

Chapter 2: Let Go of Tension

Page 18. The percentage of physicians experiencing at least one symptom of burnout was 45.5% in 2012 and 54.4% in 2015.

- Shanafelt, T.D., Hasan, O., Dyrbye, L.N., et al. (2015). Changes in burnout and satisfaction with work-life balance in physicians and the general U.S. working population between 2011 and 2014. *Mayo Clinic Proceedings, 90(12)*, 1600–1613.

Page 19. I developed the "let the center of your breathing sink" exercise when I was meditating and inwardly scanning my body for signs of stress. I noted that my breathing seemed to be centered in the lower part of my chest, and remembered that diaphragmatic breathing tended to make me more relaxed. So I "let the center of my breathing sink" and was pleasantly surprised to find that it worked very well at relaxing my whole body even more than it already was.

Page 20. Biofeedback can help people learn to lower blood pressure, heart rate and stress, and improve many other physiological measures.

- Swartz, M.S. Collura, T.F., Kamiya, J., & Swartz, N.M. (2017). The history and definitions of biofeedback and applied psychophysiology (pp 3–23). In Schwartz, M.S. & Andrasik, F. (Eds.), *Biofeedback: A practitioner's guide*, 4th edition. New York: Guilford Press.

Page 23. Chronic stress affects HRV in complicated ways that are associated with medical outcomes.

- Schubert, C., Lambertz, M., Nelesen, R.A., Bardwell, W., Choi, J.B. & Dimsdale, J.E. (2009). Effects of stress on heart rate complexity – a comparison between short-term and long-term stress. *Biological Psychology, 80(3)*, 325–332.

Pages 23–24. Several years ago, I outlined a variety of cardiovascular risk factors affected by mindful practice and other mind-body techniques.

- Bellg, A.J. (2008). Cardiovascular disease. In Boyer, B.A. and Paharia, M.I. (Eds.), *Comprehensive handbook of clinical health psychology*. Hoboken, NJ: John Wiley & Sons.

Pages 24–25. Whole-body progressive muscle relaxation (PMR) or Jacobson progressive relaxation is a powerful way of extending the benefits of the basic practice. Many people find it the most powerful exercise in this book.

Chapter 3: Reduce Distractibility

Pages 31–33. I developed the "move your fingers with your breath" and "move your arms and hands with your breath" exercises directly out of my experience with t'ai chi. Many of the people I worked with had the same difficulty learning a meditation practice as I did, and were just as frustrated. After experimenting over several years with different ways of moving and tensing muscles in sync with breathing, these two exercises seemed to be the most useful and easiest to learn. Feel free to try other ways of moving in sync with breathing to reduce distractions (for instance, when lying down, moving your toes gently in sync with your breath works well).

Page 33. Breathing through the palm of the hand placed over the lower belly is what I sometimes call an "intervention level" exercise. It's not just about eliminating distractions, but about getting a swift release of tension or anxiety when we're highly stressed, distressed and overwhelmed. Besides recommending it to many of my patients, I've used it successfully with a person sitting next to me on an airplane who was anxious about flying, relatives and others recovering from surgery, and even with psychologist colleagues having a stressful day.

Page 35–36. It is well-established that mindful practice can significantly reduce pain.

- Banth, S. & Ardebil, M.D. (2015). Effectiveness of mindfulness meditation on pain and quality of life of patients with chronic low back pain. *International Journal of Yoga, 8(2),* 128–133.

Mindful practice also improves our ability to function when we have chronic pain that can't be fully eliminated.

- Garland, E.L., Thomas, E. & Howard, M.O. (2014). Mindfulness-oriented recovery enhancement ameliorates the impact of pain on self-reported psychological and physical function among opioid-using chronic pain patients. *Journal of Pain Symptom Management, 48(6),* 1091–1099.

Chapter 4: Practice Everywhere

Page 41. Doing the daily practice in different locations and at different times may disrupt the routine of it and may also put our regular practice at risk. Regular practice comes first! But one way to look at practicing everywhere is as a backup to our usual practice. If we typically practice in the morning but have to skip it for some reason, we can find a few minutes later in the day to do the basic practice.

Page 44. Mindful walking is a wonderfully effective way to do mindful practice. It also takes no additional time out of the day. The hard part is remembering to do it, and being conscious and willing to set aside our usual distractions as we're walking from one place to another. If we can fold it into a regular routine of walking or exercise, we're there. And it's so effective that if I had to choose only one practice to do regularly, it would be this.

Page 46. Some people find that taking one or two mindful breaths throughout the day in low-stress situations is one of their favorite ways to practice.

Chapter 5: Make Mindful Choices

Page 52. The "two mindful breaths" exercise came out of what I saw my physician and nurse friends doing to compose themselves in stressful situations at work. They told me that they were "pausing to take a breath before going into a patient's room," and in that brief action, they were clearing their mind and relaxing for a moment. Then they naturally took another breath as they entered the room with a positive focus for the patient they were about to see. Quite brilliant of them!

Page 54. Repeating a word silently during meditation is very similar to the practice of centering prayer. If you wish to explore how the simple mindful practice described here can become part of a deeper spiritual practice, I encourage you to read what Fr. Thomas Keating and others say about Centering Prayer at https://www.contemplativeoutreach.org.

Chapter 6: Toward a Mindful Life

Page 59. Our understanding of the "fight-flight-freeze" response has been thoughtfully expanded by UCLA researcher Dr. Shelly Taylor, who added the concept of the "tend and befriend" response, a relationship-based approach to threats and stress that works for women in particular (and men as well).

Pages 61–63. The four humane ways of being that become easier to cultivate after mindful practice (being patient, accepting things as they are, offering kindness, and keeping things in perspective; and there are more, of course) are in part inspired by Dr. Kristen Neff's three-part definition of self-compassion (cited earlier). Her work adds an important and effective dimension to stress management, making it clear that it is not enough just to lower our stress responses. In addition to these four, there are also many other positive ways of being that can be cultivated in mindful practice. We need to acknowledge and respect ourselves and others who are suffering and in need of kindness and support.

A final note. I have been leading a weekly "Loving Acceptance" meditation during the Wednesday lunch hour for over nine years. You are welcome to join us in person or in spirit between 12:15 and 12:45 (Central Time), wherever you are. You can also listen to our meditation on Soundcloud.com, and there's a description of what we do here:

> LifePathGroup.org/mindful-practice/html

About the Author

ALBERT BELLG, Ph.D. is a writer, health psychologist, and retreat facilitator with the Center for Courage & Renewal. In one-on-one sessions and group retreats, he serves professionals, caregivers and other people looking for clarity and courage in their work and personal lives. He has practiced and taught various forms of meditation and mindful practice for over 40 years.

A graduate of Oberlin College, Dr. Bellg received his Ph.D. in Clinical Psychology from the University of Rochester in New York. He was a faculty member at Rush Medical College in Chicago, and did clinical work and research with heart patients at the Rush Heart Institute and the Appleton Heart Institute in Wisconsin. He is also a former President of the Wisconsin Psychological Association.

In addition, Dr. Bellg is a poet, the author of a book on soccer tactics, and co-author with Dr. Bruce Rybarczyk of *Listening to Life Stories: A New Approach to Stress Intervention in Health Care (Springer, 1997; Sloan Press, 2017)*. Prior to becoming a psychologist, he was a public radio producer at KCUR-FM in Kansas City, and received a Corporation for Public Broadcasting Award for one of the first locally produced public radio programs distributed nationally by satellite, *Thresholds of Science*. He also wrote speeches and training programs for the Atlanta business community.

www.ingramcontent.com/pod-product-compliance
Lightning Source LLC
Chambersburg PA
CBHW030455010526
44118CB00011B/948